tabula rasa

POETRY BY WOMEN

Published by Linen Press, London 2023
8 Maltings Lodge
Corney Reach Way
London W4 2TT
www.linen-press.com

© Linen Press 2023

The right of Linen Press to be identified as the author of this work has been asserted by her in accordance with the Copyright, Designs and Patents Act 1988.

Editors: Rawaa Elsir, Kavita A. Jindal, Avril Joy, Lynn Michell, Reshma Ruia

Individual poems remain the copyright of the poet.

All rights reserved. This book is sold subject to the condition that it shall not, by way of trade or otherwise, be lent, resold, hired out, or otherwise circulated without the publisher's prior consent in any form of binding or cover other than that in which it is published and without a similar condition, including this condition, being imposed on the subsequent purchaser.

A CIP catalogue record for this book is available from the British Library.

Cover design: Ella Piazzi
Cover image: Canva
Typeset by Zebedee
Printed by Lightning Source
ISBN: 978-1-7391777-2-0

CONTENTS

FEARLESS Ali Rowland	5
MY MOTHER WITH SWEET PEAS Clare Best	6
HOW TO BEGIN Reshma Ruia	7
CLAY ANIMALS Rachel Badger	8
GHOSTWRITER Jess Richards	9
DAUGHTER Khadija Rouf	10
THE MAGIC COAT Pen Avey	11
THE SACK RACE Karin Andrews Jashapara	12
SPLIT ENDS Alexandra Fössinger	13
THE TALKING DRESS Jess Richards	14
THE WAITING ROOM Mary-Jane Holmes	16
ACCESSORY Melanie Higgs	17
OUR CHILDREN'S CHILDHOODS Charlotte Gann	18
FOUNDLING Elizabeth Barrett	19
MEETING AT THE WATER Bernadette Gallagher	20
AT ELEPHANT MOUNTAIN Kavita A. Jindal	21
ALLOTMENT Kathleen Jones	22
WINCHESTER S.J. Litherland	23
LETTER TO MY WEDDING DRESS Avril Joy	24
THE EASE OF THINGS Anna Barker	25
YOU ARE HERE Sheena Joughin	26
GARRULUS GLANDARIUS Maria Jastrzębska	28
TEXT Deborah Morgan	29
NOTHING Ann Oakley	30
UNBOUND FEET Mona Dash	31
SECOND-CLASS PERSON Ann Oakley	32
THE NIGHT I RETURN TO MY BIRTHPLACE Deborah Morgan	33

MILESTONES Crystal Z. Lee	34
PEBBLES Holly Snaith	36
YEW Diane Cockburn	37
BEYOND THE GATE Clare Best	38
CLEARING THE ALLOTMENT Gillie Griffin	40
CALENDAR Keren Dibbens-Wyatt	41
LEAVING VARANASI Avril Joy	42
BEFORE TIMES Victoria Maynard	43
AWAITING ADORATION Kavita A. Jindal	44
WHERE ONCE HAD BEEN A WOMAN Gerry Stewart	45
SLIPPING AWAY Ali Rowland	46
JACQUELINE S.J. Litherland	48
SOMEONE IS OUT IN THE SNOW Avril Joy	50
LIMINAL Eleanor Westwood	51
EGG Reshma Ruia	52
WHEN I CONSIDER EVERYTHING THAT GROWS Gerry Stewart	53
KNITTING DAYS Bernadette Gallagher	54
VINTAGE Irene Garrow	55
ONE SMALL PROBLEM Sheena Joughin	56
DINOSAURS Marilyn Longstaff	57
WAKE IN TIME Alexandra Fössinger	58
MURMURATION, OTMOOR, 2021 Khadija Rouf	59
SUNFLOWERS Gillie Griffin	60
PETITION Mary-Jane Holmes	61
POETS	62
ACKNOWLEDGEMENTS	68

FEARLESS

Today shall we not be frightened
of all those frightening things
glowering at us from every corner
of life, electronic, physical and soulful.
Shall we instead meet along the rip tide,
let ourselves be carried away like
the little plastic boats that are tossed around
on a wind and a wave, on spindrift,
endlessly propelled towards the shore
on an interminable, repeating loop.

How deep are we in this metaphor of fearfulness?
So far that we can emerge on the other side of it,
washed clean and salty and free
of attention to it, just for a while.

Ali Rowland

MY MOTHER WITH SWEET PEAS

She couldn't bear formality,
didn't want bouquets or wreaths.
She heaped loose sweet peas
on his small white box
and when the men in slate suits
carried him into the chapel, the flowers fell
and scattered across the black floor –
violet, pink, indigo, deep velvet purple –
their sweetness drifting on the Devon air.
It's her memory, not mine.
Later she gathered the sweet peas,
took them home, strewed them on her bed,
in his cot. She said the white ones
edged with inky mauve were sweetest.
In a day or two the petals dried to tissue,
fine as skin; she filled the house again –
jars of fresh sweet peas
in every room. All summer
she brought in their scent and colour.
When there were no more sweet peas,
she slept. This is her memory.
After that she never bought or grew them
but if she caught the scent
in a florist's shop or garden,
she was back in that long summer,
her boy just gone.

Clare Best

HOW TO BEGIN

There are different ways to begin.
You stand at the doorstep, hands cupping your eyes like binoculars,
examine the rhododendron bush, the wooden fence,
the gap-toothed open gate. You remind them.
You can walk out when you wish.

Inside, you walk from room to room.
Finger the jacquard curtains in the lounge; the cushions that smell
of a husband long gone. There poses your granny, coy in a sari
inside a silver-frame photo. You've loved and left them all.
Greedy for life with your bold red-lipsticked mouth.

You sit at the kitchen table and inspect your hands,
each crevice and bump is a topographic map.
That little scar just below the joint from when you tried
to pull your wedding ring off. These are your mother's hands
pointing at you. You have failed her. So what.

Upstairs in the bathroom you strip.
Run your hands over your hips.
Across the belly where the birth scars run deep.
Your flesh puckered and brown like
mushrooms gone soft in the sun.
You cradle your heart like the babies
you carried and lost. In the mirror, you repeat.
Your voice loud like a bell.
I will begin. Again.

Reshma Ruia

CLAY ANIMALS

It was not the unfurling of the spine to walk upright,
Or the first chuckle to escape primate lungs,
Nor was it the first lips to crescent into a smile,
Passing joy between hearts.

It was not tools or spears or fire.
Cloaks of matted fur slumped over broad shoulders
Did not make us human.

It was just this:

When a plump-fingered child with red-stained palms
Was lifted onto shoulders
One hand cradling a parent's ear for balance,
Shaping her world into a rock,
Semaphoring us through time.

Rachel Badger

GHOSTWRITER

Jess Richards

DAUGHTER

She emerged. Tiny prophet, wrapped in scarlet silks,
smeared in an opal sheen of vernix, but held
by a leathery cord, turquoised with unbreath.
Connected like an aquanaut to her mothership.

Tiny survivor, scooped into a midwife's hands.
Held up: dazed starfish, now heavy with gravity,
stranded at the margins of my comprehension,
foretelling my changed life with her hungry mouth.

Determined, needy, desperate to live – flailing her arms,
chewing her fists. Tiny mammal, snuffling and mewing.
I slipped my hand under her leaf-light bones,
felt her whole length in my palm –

the knuckly cogs of her spine in outline
tucked her close close   close to my flesh
hidden in my eyes, embroidered in my breath
I pitched at the thought of my power, afraid.

But when her sage eyes opened, ancient-faced
as if she'd slept a thousand years
as if she had the wisdom of the universe
but had no language to tell what she knew.

Her first look at me, her eyes grey blue
slowly blinking, her look of mild surprise.
That look stoked the blaze and fury of protection,
beyond my lifetimes: recognition. She saw me

newborn and naked. I was latched and locked
within her gaze. And everything
I thought I knew
about my 'self', quietly slipped away.

Khadija Rouf

THE MAGIC COAT

Me, a little girl aged six.

Sifting seconds from richer cousins. Rifling through, while sister May
    pouts, 'Nothing fits!'
I offer up a gappy grin.
'More for me then.'

'Try these jeans, this top, those boots,' says Mum, puffing on a fag.
A rag-tag fashion show begins. May laughs through her hand because
my top's on back to front.

Diving into trashy treasure, I catch my breath as flashy red shouts out
    from under muted grey. May snatches up a scarlet pea coat: fur-trimmed
    hood and silver buttons.
I brim with fiery triumph when the narrow cuffs cut circulation.

Wrapped in silk-lined cherry richness, flushed face twinning crimson wool
and polyester mix.
Mum and May gape as I twirl.

That winter, strangers stop us in the street, remarking on my grace and
    style. I smile,
serene, from deep within the hooded warmth.
Radiant.

Next winter, howling in frustration because my special coat has shrunk.
I plead with Mum to buy another;
she shakes her head while sly May smirks.

These days I've lost that gap-toothed grin, but when I slick red lipstick on
reflected in my mirror mind –
a six-year-old in her magic coat.

Pen Avey

THE SACK RACE

For years I ran the sack-race
clutching its rough rim
hobbling fast with
small sacky steps.

Like this sack was my skin,
firebird flying alongside
egging me on. But once I stumbled
to laughter and applause
and tumbled deeper in:
a tiny self in the cavernous sack
rough burlap and brindled dark.

In an earthy-scented tunnel I found
a thin little saint, couched
in grainy gloom,
tinkling with facial safety-pins,
fresh from hunger-strike.

'Don't be afraid' I said.
'No!' she croaked soft
'we had our dashing lives –
all that we chased and loved
and fought for. Scattered shards.

Rest now, we must find our songs, and sing them.'
But we stayed silent there, releasing all regrets,
that chilly, owlish night, till light trickled back
into the rough weaving.

Karin Andrews Jashapara

SPLIT ENDS

I saw a woman today,
she was wearing my coat
and I wondered
would she be willing
to take over my skin as well?
It's only half of one of
the many possible lives –

Sirena bifida
with a chainsaw.
All my books were lost
in the great fire; hear

the sweet hereafter calling
louder and louder.

Alexandra Fössinger

THE TALKING DRESS

            Hang me on a wardrobe door
lie on the bed with your lover—
        —hide the belly you believe is too wide
without me, you unpick your body—
              —into despicable parts
earlier tonight at the party I was complimented—
        —*a beautiful dress… so exquisite*, you gleamed
now I no longer enclose you—
           —you are in pieces all over again
hide one leg beneath the other; the pupils—
             —of your eyes turn dark
my zip nipped at the neck your lover kisses—
     —does skin against skin feel like velvet, cotton, silk,
or the scrape of scissors—
    —there's jealousy in my creases while your thighs rise and fall
but you don't watch your lover; you watch me.

           —Was I a boundary, your border
(though my seams hold me together) —
              —separating
your skin from stranger—
      —bodies? Flood your hair over the pillow,
drown beneath the sheet—
            —while your lover comes
then sleeps. When you rise—
       —the pillow exhales, the sheet twists away—
I murmur *come to me alone and stroke me gently*—
    —you whisper, *I took sewing classes, just to make you fit*
these breasts, arms, waist, thighs—
   —*identical shop-racks are designed for identical rack-people*
you step inside and zip me up, hook tooth into tooth—
          —run heartbeats through me
like your thudding silver needle—
       —thump, through facing and double-seams
thump, through warp and weft—
        —I feel you longing for more textures
for wafting weight—
          —and warped weightlessness

torn expanses of an ever-fraying sky—
                              —for interchangeable layers of thick
and thin—
—skin.

Jess Richards

THE WAITING ROOM

On this island, there are trees that bear fruit like women, with shapes, bodies, eyes, hands, feet, hair, breasts, and vulvas like the vulvas of women. They are the most beautiful of face and hang by their hair…when they feel the wind and sun, they yell, 'Waq Waq, [help help] until their hair tears apart. When their hair tears, they die. Ibn al-Wardi *(d.1348)*

We sit – an atoll of women – gently
metastasising like slow-to-ripen fruit
beneath the strip-lighted pulse
of this wave-filled coast, archipelago
of scan, x-ray, magnetic resonance.

In this forest's bloom, we wait, hollow
as calabash, thumbing mounds of *Vogue*
and other fabulas of paradise that recount
little of how to stem lava flows or build
boats out of small pieces of wood.

The world flits around us in coral scrubs
and Crocs, exotic birds singing out
our names, our dates of birth, clocking
our descent in cubits of hair length
while we learn what it is to be marooned

to forever button, unbutton our clothes
until we are just a back-lit negative of tree
shadows on a chart, sum of our disposable
parts: stroma, lobule, areola, ovary, bone
lymph, breath, wind, sun, the roar of a full moon.

Mary-Jane Holmes

ACCESSORY

I was promenaded in a pram,
a navy-blue and cream number
my mother imported from London.
Dad was only flying weekends
in the reserves. Sometimes, they had cereal
for dinner, and there was a lodger
named Stan, from Poland.
But she was styling on the seawall
in her pencil skirt and heels,
me bouncing along,
above the huge, spoked wheels.

When I was thirteen, she gave me *The Prophet*.
I devoured it, my bedroom turned poet's garret,
my heart blooming with the deep meaning of it all.

One day, I was told to peel potatoes for dinner.
'Your children are not your children.
They come through you but not from you…'
I quoted at her. 'Nonsense!'
She stuck her head out from the pantry,
'You are my biggest achievement
and every inch my doing.'

It's true that I can peel a potato
faster than most.

Melanie Higgs

OUR CHILDREN'S CHILDHOODS

It was a hard, cold, wet slog, that climb.
We were heading away from shelter

talking as we walked, skirting around
our scariest subjects: when we didn't love

enough, when we loved too much.
Our whole children's histories stretched out

behind us now. Those years we'd meet
each week to escape and laugh. And now this.

When we got to the top we were at least
rewarded: sun, a rainbow, the huge

vista, a field of mustard, windmill. We sat
and shivered on our wet cagoules on the edge

of everything, drank the beer we'd each
brought with us, ate our cheese and onion crisps.

I cried then, when I said how completely
my son seemed to have left me – and as we

descended our pace quickened; I turned the talk
to Netflix. Did not say, how can we stay

with our discomfort, which is what I really
wanted to ask you, friend, but couldn't.

Charlotte Gann

FOUNDLING

The mothers left prin ted birds and acorns
butterflies and flower s
on cuffs of cherryder ry and lawn,
flannel and linsey tor n from their petticoats.
A ribbon or piece of gown was bound
into a billet book for the foundling child.
One woman stitched her son's initials
in red worsted on thi s frayed swatch.
If you could match t he piece
you could reclaim yo ur child.
I imagine a mother b urying
half a camblet heart i n a drawer,
tacking a scrap of pa duasoy silk
into the lining of her bra.
There is no ledger fo r my token.
Nowhere to record m y daughter's
distinguishing marks or the clothes
she was wearing whe n I last saw her
(purple converse, den im jeans, a mole
on her abdomen, scar on her left knee).
A foundling mother I rummage
through off-cuts in m y sewing box.
Here is her name em broidered
in green on cream co tton tape,
a silver butterfly snip ped from a purse,
her first stitches in re d aida.
I choose a yellow rib bon printed
with narcissi. I tear t he fairing,
pin half to my pillow.

Elizabeth Barrett

MEETING AT THE WATER

We meet at the well,
the stream, the shore –
to wash ourselves, our clothes.

At Babylon I saw you
bent over at your work,
chatting, then resting against a tree.

I saw you in Darjeeling
sitting on your throne
of sacks, waiting

at the well, amongst women,
young and not so, with bare feet
and hands under cold water

you made us clean –
we didn't know we needed
your absolution.

Bernadette Gallagher

AT ELEPHANT MOUNTAIN

Las Alpujarras

Late-settling dusk turns to evening cool
a half moon and one star appear
as do the ladies of the village
in their loose dresses

they sit out on the street, gossip
let their dogs bark at passers-by

On our terrace we pass around
a snifter of local brandy
inhaling our wishes
exhaling polite smiles

Next evening the moon slides up behind
the curved back of Elephant Mountain

casts its silver light into my room
calls me to my window mesh
to bathe in its luminescence
to be blessed in silence.

Kavita A. Jindal

ALLOTMENT

*It's curtains for the traditional allotment
as women move in.* The Telegraph

This is my pitch – ten Anglo-Saxon poles –
in which I practise the art of double-digging
feeling the smooth slice of the spade's travel
through the reluctant loam.

I have left the abandoned parsnips
to feather and flower a foot above my head
as my spade amputates forgotten beetroot
and potatoes, part of last year's glut.

Grandpa kept a bucket in his shed
to piss in. Well-matured, it fertilised
the celery and rhubarb. Nothing so personal here –
just bone meal and chicken shit
and a compost heap swarming with ants.

My neighbour's strip has cabbages
centred with stick and string, and straight rows
of onions standing to attention as if shocked,
as he is, by such disorderly abundance.

But in the dusk, in the rain, crouching
to weed the seedling salad patch
my fingers brown and swollen
with nettle stings, I realise that this
is where I was always meant to be –

replicating the actions of Viking wives
crouched in their small garths, beside fjords,
and all those other northern women, after the ice,
bedding down in caves and turf-roofed crannogs

sowing wild grain, transplanting berry bushes,
coaxing supper out of stony ground.

Kathleen Jones

WINCHESTER

Streets unwove as we walked
                    medieval unwinding
to the cathedral heart, *the shop we entered*,

        I am wearing now the earrings
of rose quartz (like sweets in sucked roundness)

        I sought to pair with a favoured necklace
a bargain for a fiver
                    the one I never wear

    its clusters of rose quartz unliked, the pairing
too absolute. *Your pleasure in my find*

pins the moment   my unsought happiness
     at the chance of a match
                    blessed the day
of walking through cloisters
                    coming across
unknown cathedral quarters

the day returns as I pick pink globes encased
in silver, *your glee, your willingness*
                    to share a small joy
that expanded effortlessly.

What we keep and what we discard
                    is unknown.
The pairing did not last, but the day
in Winchester
            stays encased in our friendship.
The day unwove
            as we looked into the window
the memory unwinding
            to the heart's archive.

S.J. Litherland

LETTER TO MY WEDDING DRESS

I might have worn you with my hair long, like Joni Mitchell
hidden something in periwinkle under your skirt, carried cornflowers

cut you on the cross, a tea gown all satin and Hollywood
I might have felt you brush my skin like a cobweb smelling of morning

kept you, wrapped in ancient, yellowing tissue to show you
to a daughter, to show you how young, how small I was

then, or thrown you in the dressing up box, or trashed you, yes
there is a fashion now for trashing your wedding dress with mud

or paint and taking photographs. I might have managed with
what I had, trailing you across the music room floor, where the boards

creaked and the piano caught the mood, that's when I missed you most.
I make you over a thousand times, sew you myself, spin you

from dream but there is always something missing, the flowers
uncollected, wilting, a muslin toile without its sleeve…

Avril Joy

THE EASE OF THINGS

Feel the old bones
on their way to ash, the cat shit,
the blind worm.

The pull of roots, the lost marble,
the inert bulbs whispering
what they could've been.

The hold of clay.
The rotting mulch
still warm with the life

of the flower,
the leaf.
Green shoots.

Not inconceivable
something could grow
from all this.

That I might one day
stand up,
wipe my hands clean.

Know better the ease of things.

Anna Barker

YOU ARE HERE

for Simon

We peer to scan the map
that heralds the pebbled path
and with our fingers trace a route
towards the hidden beach
we hope to reach
this dubious afternoon...

Your legs being
longer than mine
you stop from time to time;
you sit, admire the view
then I catch up with you...

We move on again
to find ourselves deciding
that this countryside
is kind. We don't mind the rain
that squalls towards the beach
which we might almost reach
this August afternoon...

When my ankle
twists, it rankles you –
(I must be careful of myself)
You smoke a cigarette.
We rest. You pass a battered flask.

You see three boats
against the sky
and point them out
then loudly count –
but I see only two, although I strain
to look and look (but where?) again.

We share some squares of chocolate
as I wonder if it matters
that what we see together
is hardly ever the same.

Sheena Joughin

GARRULUS GLANDARIUS

When the jay comes, swooping down into our small garden
   Quick! I mouth. She's outwitted

the pigeons which crowd her, their feathers puffed up.
   Electric blue bars on her wings dazzle –

mirroring sky somewhere far, as if a forest had flown in
   screeching. When the jay comes

I imagine she has left her nest, risking everything to snatch
   some sustenance. *How do you carry on?*

Does it make your voice shrill, the years being ridiculed?
   When the jay comes, a blur of pinkish brown,

I never get a chance to tell her how clever she is mimicking
   hawks to sound fiercer.

*Does it work to open your beak wider ready to kill
   when you're attacked?*

There are so many questions I wish I could ask her.
   Instead I wave you over to the window.

Quick! It's the jay! Electric blue bars on her wings
   dazzle – mirroring another sky.

We grip hands tightly when the jay comes, swooping down
   among our sweet peas, her name close to joy.

Maria Jastrzębska

TEXT

I love the sound tyres make on a dry road,
have pulled over, eyes shut, trying to determine
the direction of every passing vehicle.

Your last text, how I make you cringe,
how the thought of being with me
makes you want to be elsewhere, made me cry.

The speed of what must be a lorry rattles my car,
and I'm a seed in an apple, dark and narrow,
a half-closed eye, eased out with a knife,

tossed away, taken on a journey
I could never have imagined, not even now,
with everything passing.

Deborah Morgan

NOTHING

I am a figment of your imagination
just someone you dreamt up
to keep you company
on this broken road
of a journey we never chose
but have to take

because the alternative is worse
I mean of course unknown

better the devil you know
do you know what I mean?

here we are then
not in the middle way
but near the end
and I am tired of your fictions
why can't you understand
why can't you see me as I am?

nothing, I am nothing, you see

I am a hand resting on the rotting grave
the black hole of an unseen star
I am the skeleton of a funfair tunnel
so you don't need to bother with me after all

I am no-one's mother or lover
in fact no person of any substance at all
it would be quite wrong to see me
as a woman with a room of her own

Ann Oakley

UNBOUND FEET

First they bound our feet,
bones shattered, chicken-wing dust post-dinner,
flesh putrefied, perfumed, placed in lavish silk shoes,
so small, so beautiful, butterfly feet
that cannot stand firm, that cannot run
battered, warped
lily-feet

then they learnt to not bind our feet
but when we ran, they laughed
when we tried to stand firm, the earth was pulled away
craters and venom beneath
boulders tied to feet, pushed into the soil
a living burial

they don't always have to try hard
the cages they grow us in
the boxes they stifle us in

breaking our bodies and our breath
so they don't have to.

Mona Dash

SECOND-CLASS PERSON

O woman chasing a cancelled train
why on earth should I suppose
you intended to travel first class?
I, a simple man in scarlet uniform
just doing my duty, marooned
in ordinary assumptions, festooned
with the usual emblems of patriarchy

for yes, I am one of them
quite low down on the scale, I admit
but proud of my position all the same
from which you seem to me
merely a little old woman
with grey hair and a second-class ticket
scurrying for a train in the early morning
and therefore not someone of importance
with first-class business to transact

Ann Oakley

THE NIGHT I RETURN TO MY BIRTHPLACE

fingers, dainty, rattling through
the stitches around my mother's mouth
the jail I grew up in will have no lock
nor key, the ants that lived and died
in the vinegar bottle will no longer
climb onto the old wooden table
there will be books given back
to me from bins, by Jimmy,
our caretaker, there will be wolves
in the caretaker, there will be wolves
in the tenements, circling our flats
piling up the corpses of all those
who beat their children, beat
their wives, the women will spend
their family allowance on food
instead of it being stolen for booze
my grandmother will not curse but
sing climbing the stone steps home,
Way, hay hay, Sweet Molly Malone.

Deborah Morgan

MILESTONES

Zero. I came with nothing not even a mother. Ma, the angel
passing through passing on. A blink of memory, scintilla of light

9. Hunched over a fire, sparks in the darkness. Cooking for little brother
who Ba said could eat the eggs that I wasn't allowed

16. Met the pockmarked man. Obey, said Ba and the matchmaker. The
    gold miner
spoke Mandarin Japanese Taiwanese. Sheets soaked in a sea, my tears

18. Married a man twice my age. A dutiful daughter, a good Chinese
wife. Truth uncovered. He was a miner, but the colonizers owned the
    mines

20. Blamed for our son's condition. Knocked to the ground, bruised
to my knees. In 1945 the Japanese colonizers fled Taiwan, the mines
    looted

36. birthday candles she insisted. She was at the age when I stopped
    schooling
started cooking. Books, stacks for my daughter even if her father threw
    them at me

42. yet looked decades on. Maybe from long hours at the factory or from
    hospital
stays with my son or from the beating

50. Daughter's wedding in Taipei. Disapproved of the poor professor, he
    granted
neither gift nor blessing. I had enough
saved, enough for their new life
at the university in America

55. Leave Ba, it's time, Daughter said. What about your brother, I thought

63. Mourned son's passing all year, a sweet child
trapped in a man's body, he never hurt anybody. Can't fathom
he was his father's son

78. The brain will wipe the slate clean, doctors said. Daughter wept,
      moved in, said
Don't forget me, I'll remind you everyday

82 or 83 or 96 or 104. Phantoms or angels. I see
my children my joy my stars my moon my bones. I see Ma
blinking, floating, flying, fleeting
scintillating shadows of lights.

Crystal Z. Lee

PEBBLES

And so you shaped yourself into perfect
Round, soft, palm-flattened pebbles
All piled atop one another like a wall,
Strong, steadfast, unwilling to yield
Whenever the storm broke upon you.
But others came along and took a stone
Here and there, just for keepsakes, or
To make your facade more appealing
Or to polish them up until they shone,
Because they knew that to grind a facet
Or two would make you more perfect
So that you better fit into their hands.
Yet you hold fast against the incursions
That loosen you, that take from you
Who you are, and lay more pebbles
Atop your crest so that one day someone
Will rest their head against your crags
And simply be glad that you still stand.

Holly Snaith

YEW

'It's dangerous,' she says, stroking her arm up and down
because she has goosepimples just mouthing the word dangerous.
He holds out the yew berries, bright shocking pink in their little cups,
picks one out, placing it delicately on his tongue.

She watches him roll it around his mouth and then he is nibbling
the flesh off it, spitting out the seed. Laughing at her.
'Delicious. Go on. I dare you.'

She turns away towards the tree, thick and dark, glossy needles black,
    green,
the ground beneath bare. No light.
Takes a berry and bites into it. Sweet, sticky. Another, and another.

He walks to the gate, and she follows him.
Next, they are going to look for dead sheep in the field,
'They explode when you poke them,' he says.

Above them thrushes are gorging on the fruit.
She hears one singing, flute-like. Over and over.
She forgets to spit out the seeds.

Diane Cockburn

BEYOND THE GATE

*in memory of Sarah Everard
and all the others*

scots pine and resin-scented air
     out here
giant oak   left of the path
     we are walking

sycamore   in sun   in shade
holly crowding ragged elder

sweet chestnut   spruce fir   douglas fir
     with us
field maple   half-uprooted beech
     out here   walking

sorbus domestica   the service tree
and elm   rare elm

blackthorn   black with sloes
     with us   out here
hawthorn   hazel   leaning ash
     and we are walking

ivy   juniper   cherry   poplar
copper beech and twisted willow

so many hornbeam   so many birch
     out here
stripped leafless by fine sleet
     as we are   walking

ranks of cypress   sapling larch
branches creaking high above

wild plum and wild pear
        we are   we are
scarred   black-leafed   still with fruit
       walking   walking

Clare Best

CLEARING THE ALLOTMENT

Three ripe raspberries rest, cupped in my palm,
rescued from the morning's war on bindweed.
Bloodied skim of danger. A burgundy of harm

beneath the carpet vines. The thorns' sharp pain
lurked for my misstep. A reach too far, I'd bleed
like the three ripe raspberries held in my palm.

Gently, I carry them home. Proof I can tame
a tangled bed, lay bare the soil, find the seed
of bloodied danger. The burgundy of harm

is somewhere else. Nightly, I watch it. Russian stains
spread across Ukraine, while crushed hopes bleed
fragile as the raspberries cupped in my palm.

I call the allotment a bombsite. A shame
of twisted metal, rotten wood, plants waiting to be freed.
But real bloody danger, real burgundy of harm

lies far away, beyond my reach. Real bodies remain
trapped. I rescue what I can. It becomes my creed.
Those three ripe raspberries cupped in my palm.
Plucked from the skim of danger, the burgundy of harm.

Gillie Griffin

CALENDAR

there is a day waiting
for me and my paintbox
left unmarked
I don't want to spoil the square
or jinx the hope

when it comes
I will fall into its silent folds
of clean cotton
done laundry
and fresh fabric

sit in blank awe
before its canvas
sigh my colours
around its edges
letting the crisp snowy centre
hold my remains

Keren Dibbens-Wyatt

LEAVING VARANASI

At dusk I climb the stairs to the top of the house
look out over salt marsh to the sea folding
laundry, shirts, old towels, worn sheets.

Swifts dive over marram grass
over water rills horned poppies lean
from a wind sprung and leaking at the sills.

And the boats are going out now, the ten-ups
red lights bobbing and flickering, mapping
sea from shore and it's as if I am out

with them, floating in the darkness. Alive.
Ready to stay up all night and watch the morning come
like we did in the jungle, cycling until dawn

through firefly and rice paddy to the bus station
where we boarded a bus, half-empty
windows blown, leaving Varanasi

the promise and wandering of youth, panning
for gold sieving oceans and continents, staying up
long after we should, coming in with the boats.

Avril Joy

BEFORE TIMES

I got here with thumb-printed wax,
So green all over, too soft to handle.
The middling years of my youth look like they belonged
To somebody else. And somehow they did. But before all of that,
I ran up a hill. And this hill was endless, tired, all of twelve years.
It ate up the forest, so when the leaves fell down they didn't get to fall,
Just floated like stars in that wide, wide blue, soft-thick of the prairie,
That low wash of heat burned sun-white and sleeping. When that wax
    was warm,
The forest was steaming: the mist walked over
From where they could see it, what I couldn't see.
But I didn't need to know. Tears seeped past me, slow and irrelevant.
Sometimes I feel them in sea-taste at night, all salt in my nose. But
Mostly I think I just want to be one of them, ancient and looming,
No secret trick. As strong and as easy as
Leaving your eyes open, leaving your arms open, not bearing night at all.

Victoria Maynard

AWAITING ADORATION

If I'm sent back
I want to be
a black-cap warbler

enticing
a slumbering woman
into a wakeful joyous morning.

Or part of a mountain peak
thrust into a lowering sky
awaiting for millennia
climbers
and awestruck adoration.

Kavita A. Jindal

WHERE ONCE HAD BEEN A WOMAN

Midnight, and if the sky is full of wishes
I missed them.
Or it was too early to hook
my story upon one's tail,
to chase the aurora
with an echo and crackle of longing.

My footsteps, a single trail
burning through the frosted grass,
crinkle and then collapse,
leaving the way to this point
meltingly clear.

Years of that crisp, straight-line feeling,
crumpled, tossed away
like scribbled paper,
losing myself in the creases.

The ice at my core unfurls,
growing impossible petals and ribbons.
I awake, a pale star
fizzing towards explosion.

Gerry Stewart

SLIPPING AWAY

When your life changes suddenly,
irrevocably, and everything is not
as you always knew it to be:
this is like the place where the land
falls suddenly away to the sea,
and everything looks as if the cliffs
will tumble at any moment, and that you would fall,
despite yourself, without a thought,
and the cold water would bubble
into all your spaces,
wanting to own your breath,
your body and your heart.

It might feel like an ending,
a wiping clean of everything.

     Or you might find yourself
standing as the cattle and sheep there do,
grazing thoughtfully,
near-vertical, but deeply unconcerned,
You may not topple, but scramble down instead,
a little crazily, a touch out of control,
to then find your feet in sand,
on a slither of beach, the narrowest refuge,
instantly distracted from your grazed skin
by the thought of bathing in a deep, calm sea.

It will take time for this more precarious world,
way out of calling distance from where you were before,
to feel familiar to you.

    Soon you might reach towards new islands,
braving the silvery rips,
and the tides become your heartbeat,
a rhythm for a new kind of life,
and some of it, at least, will be well.

Ali Rowland

JACQUELINE

High line of Acton from my window
Chiswick Empire spinning ball
the nights of roofs/ the days of attic living

could be Paris/ Jean Paul Sartre open at my table
grainy coffee a zigzag of wallpapers
intentionally breaking every rule

and calmly surveying the new order
a portrait by Picasso
presiding over passion

primary colours of red and blue
still presides in my home.
I didn't know her name was mine.

She survives two fires and a flood
my two marriages
the to-ing and fro-ing of partners

and two years of the echoing
emptiness of Covid as we look over
the end of the bed together

over the deep Vale of trees,
over the balcony doors and rail,
over a settled stillness behind glass

she turns her head aslant/ her hands folded
and wrapped one over the other
she was his last wife/ survived the mistresses.

She was my youth and womanhood.
The Roads to Freedom my textbook
and newly acquired Party Card as proof

no half measures/ but nothing cut and dried
the *avant garde* the angel on my shoulder.
I would always be on the outside, untied.

S.J. Litherland

SOMEONE IS OUT IN THE SNOW

Faintly falling the snow,
at the end of things
as in *The Dead* by Joyce,
like the tracks,
there when I push my head
through the curtains
look out onto the white road.

Faintly falling the tracks
you make across the night,
that say – you have been here
the road is passable –
though silent
no plough gone through,
as if we have given up hope
as if this new assault from the east
will penetrate bone
and propagate its dissolution.

Faintly falling your voice
cupped like a fledgling
in my hands, messages
that say – sleep now
you have done all you can.
Do not watch the world
as you once did,
thinking you could make it
a place of safety.
You cannot stop the wind
or the snow falling
someone is out this snowy night.

Avril Joy

LIMINAL

I inhabit the liminal time
the edge between night
and night-becoming-dawn
slipping like an owl's wing
between the branches of silver birch.

I inhabit the liminal in you
pausing between woman
and woman-becoming-crone
with all the shifts and
settlings this brings,
the drawing-up of
moisture so as to make a well.

I inhabit the liminal
between you and other
the part of the smile
that speaks and soars,
the part of the touch that tingles
shudders into something primal
becoming urgent, wet, creative.

And so it begins again
   in the dark
where all things begin
where the mud gives birth to the river
and the night gives birth to the sun.

Eleanor Westwood

EGG

It is at night
I hear you
A single cell you keep sucking
My vitals so noisily
Now a limb, an eye, a throat
Just don't ask me to feel
Love for you as yet my unborn child
To shut my eyes tight
And breathe your name out like a prayer
It is too early to feel
Tender towards
This accident of cells
Multiplying within
There are no grudges against you
As yet
Just this need persists
To make you understand
This body and mind
Dozing clumsy through the hours
Does not mean
There won't be far-off djinns
Waiting to be won
Urgent footsteps urging me to run
This blood will still growl
Though now it whimpers low
You won't fell me down my unborn child
With your love or your blows

Reshma Ruia

'WHEN I CONSIDER EVERYTHING THAT GROWS'

Shakespeare, Sonnet 15

old, taller or away from me,
I no longer tend and trim them back
to keep them manageable,
children like weeds
or worries climbing up the brickwork.
Hours unwind around my ankles
like the cat's unending hope
that I will open the door
until I follow them out.
Shadows lengthen the garden,
I trace their angles
deep into the grass.
Burrs catch on my legs,
the itch of last year's memories
become this year's seeds.
Carried into the sleeping house
they'll pass between the children
from dream to dream
and take root and grow.

Gerry Stewart

KNITTING DAYS

in memoriam Bella Gallagher, 1920-1997

I hear your needles clicking, knitting a jumper
all those hanks of wool rolled into balls.

Pattern in your head, in your hands – diamonds
emerging as the sculptor carves to release the form within.

You knitted me my long red cardigan, green fleck for our son,
along with hat and scarf to match, brown for his father.

Knitting our days together
only the moths will unravel.

Bernadette Gallagher

VINTAGE

Why save jugs in orange and blue
or mushroom photos of
a dress, a smile, a cheekbone?
Rise, collect *yourself*

put the fading scarf of flowers
around your head tight,
scuff the leather shoes now
throw the books unread with dust away.

Smell lavender and roses,
pour out drinks and words,
close the door to dull
and polish the floor.

Let us dance in time,
hum long playing records,
lace a cigarette through a hand,
crack jokes as eggs unbroken

enjoy the heat, the sudden night
the eye less sharp but better.
We too will smile one day
from a curling photograph.

Irene Garrow

ONE SMALL PROBLEM

There was a pocket in our school-uniform knickers
which rumpled round white ankles as we crouched
in cold and hurried cramped conditions
of crack-mapped walls, dark lino, doors with gaps...

Maths with constipation. Monthlies. Everybody anxious
and nobody, not even the Head Girl, knowing enough
to be sure of what the pocket was for...
Were we to keep a penny in it?
Was it for tissues? An eraser? Depilatory cream?
The string we cradled cats with in the playground?
A whistle, for situations in which you couldn't scream?
Or folded paper puzzles, which we slipped inky fingers into

and asked out 'Yellow, Red or Blue or Green?'
then lifted flaps to giggle over risqué consequences?
For eye-lash glue? Your father's office number?
A mother's maiden name?

Let me explain –
That pocket had to be unfilled and flat.
No one tells small girls this fact. They have to guess
until they're grown and try to get filled up
with men and love and messiness and sex.
In retrospect we understand its perfect emptiness.

Sheena Joughin

DINOSAURS

after Epitaph by Robert Desnos

We lived in those times of grants and fees paid
we ordinary girls from poor backgrounds;
post-war optimism, the baby-boomers;
we National-Healthy girls who went
to new and red-brick universities,
each outnumbered five to one by men.
    And we weren't grateful.
And lots of us made our own clothes:
psychedelic mini-skirts, velvet loons.

We lived in those times of student revolution,
a girl on our corridor hanged herself one morning –
after her year in France, the Paris riots –
while we were *sitting in* The Great Hall,
storming the Administration, colonising
the Vice-Chancellor's office – that time of
free discos, walks back to digs at daybreak,
threats that we'd all be sent down.

How lucky we were and we didn't know it,
plenty of jobs, cheap flats, no loans, no debt
to hang round our middle-aged necks.
We dinosaurs.

Marilyn Longstaff

WAKE IN TIME

In the voice you silenced, love flees
unheard. The wakeful
soul, your gift a curse no one
took up in recognition, the spaces
in between you did not share –
save the vision of a resurfacing

place. It was underneath the ice
you learned the tragedy of growing
old is not that we grow old, but we stay
young – every day becomes a
walk from grave to womb.

Alexandra Fössinger

MURMURATION, OTMOOR, 2021

Dusk approaching, a clear sky's
covenant with frost, and the waiting,
whispering cathedral of reeds

and here is the epiphany –
sudden starlings – seen, unseen, seen –
twisting and turning their hymn

feathered liturgy, lilting
heartbeat rhythm, breathing
the biting air, in harmony

pilgrim swell of shimmering wings
curling, pulsing, swirling –
visible, invisible, visible –

ductile, conjuring shapes,
souls of the dead congregating
into a black chrysanthemum

until thrumming beats into decision
and in communion, they drop
and pour into the reed beds
like dark wine

Khadija Rouf

SUNFLOWERS

I'm planting sunflowers for sure this year.
I need to witness their sudden yellow strength:
such boldness, such height, such thickness of stem.

I'm planting sunflowers, though I may
wrap them in barbed wire and dowse them in hot sauce
chanting incantations to ward off the pesky deer.

I'm planting sunflowers for Ukraine,
so every time I look outside I'll see a line
of yellow hope, bravely walking, heads held high.

I'm planting sunflowers for Volodymyr Zelenskyy
while watching *Servant of the People* on Netflix.
He plays a history teacher, elected as President

except now he is. So, when I see him on the evening news
in a bulletproof vest, I want to laugh.
Except now he isn't funny. He looks so tired, so small.

I'm planting sunflowers for all the small Babas
filling the pockets of Russian soldiers with seeds
so where they fall, flowers will grow. Their blood will not be wasted.

I'm planting sunflowers for sure this year.
We all need their yellow strength,
their boldness, their height, their thickness of stem.

Gillie Griffin

PETITION

Let's sit a while on this Whin Sill ledge, the flesh
of afternoon warm at our backs, the bones of night
half a life ahead of us. Let's sit a while amongst
the slender cruet-moss, the round-leaved sundew,
the devil's matchsticks; unscrew the flask, unwrap
the cellophaned sandwiches whilst a church-bell away
the evening's casserole simmers on low, the tumble
dryer hums its cante jondo to misty-eyed windows.

Is this what our dead
have been trying to tell us? – that love
resides in such small actions.

Listen how the limestone sugars beneath us
Listen how the lichen grows, the gentian flowers
Listen how the hours grass over our hearts

Mary-Jane Holmes

POETS

Pen Avey writes and illustrates under the wide skies of West Norfolk. Her poetry has appeared in anthologies by Patrician Press and has been displayed, poster-sized, in railway stations as part of the 2021 Renfrewshire Mental Health Arts Festival. Find out more at penavey.com or follow her on Twitter @penavey

Rachel Badger is a language teacher from Wales who loves writing prose and poetry almost as much as she loves her cat and drinking tea.

Anna Barker has written two novels: *Floating Island* and *Before I Knew Him* as Anna Ralph (Penguin Random House) and, as Barker, a collection of short stories, *Rain Hare* (Iron Press). Her poetry has appeared, or is forthcoming, in Acumen, Humana Obscura, Typehouse, and Interpreter's House. In 2022 she won the Indigo Dreams Publishing poetry prize for her poem *My hen as my vagina, a love story*. *The Ease of Things* is from her forthcoming debut poetry collection, *Book of Crow*.

Elizabeth Barrett's collections include *A Dart of Green and Blue* (Arc Publications, 2010), *The Bat Detector* (Wrecking Ball Press, 2007) and *Walking on Tiptoe* (Staple First Editions, 1998). *Foundling* is taken from her new collection, *Falling Mother* (Wrecking Ball Press, forthcoming), for which she received a Northern Writers Award in 2018. She is currently a Royal Literary Fund Fellow at the University of Sheffield.

Clare Best is a poet, memoirist, essayist, librettist, editor and university lecturer in Creative Writing. She often collaborates with visual artists. In 2020-2021 she held a Fellowship at Guildhall School of Music & Drama, working with composers and artists to create operas and other vocal works. Her latest publication is the bilingual pamphlet *End of Season / Fine di stagione* (Frogmore Press 2022) clarebest.co.uk

Diane Cockburn is a surrealist Northern Irish poet living and working in Durham. Her collection, *Electric Mermaid*, is published by Arrowhead Press. The title poem was shortlisted for the Forward Prize. Her pamphlet, *Under Surveillance*, is published by Vane Women Press.

Mona Dash is the winner of The Asian Writer 2018 and lives in London. She writes fiction and poetry. Her memoir, *A Roll of the Dice: A Story of Loss, Love and Genetics* won the Eyelands Book Award. Her short story collection, *Let Us Look Elsewhere*, was shortlisted for the 2018 SI Leeds Literary Prize (Dahlia Books, 2022).

Keren Dibbens-Wyatt is a chronically-ill contemplative writer and artist. She has a passion for prayer, poetry, story and colour. Her writing regularly features in literary journals (*Fathom, Amethyst Review, The Blue Nib*) and spiritual blogs (*Contemplative Light, Godspace*). She is the author of *Recital of Love* (Paraclete Press, 2020) and *Young Bloody Mary* (Mogzilla Books, 2023). kerendibbenswyatt.com

Alexandra Fössinger is a German/Italian native speaker from Italy. She is the author of the poetry collection *Contrapasso* (Cephalopress, 2022). Her work is published in numerous journals, including Tears *in the Fence, The Frogmore Papers, Wild Court, High Window, Mono, La Piccioletta Barca,* and *Reliquiae*. She is interested in the spaces between things, the tiny shifts in time, the overlooked, the unsaid.

Bernadette Gallagher is a poet from Donegal living in County Cork. She is a recipient of The Arts Council of Ireland Agility Award (2021). Her poetry is published in, among others, *Agenda, The Stinging Fly, The North, Stony Thursday, The Frogmore Papers, Dreich, Southword, University College Dublin Poetry Archive* and *Words Lightly Spoken* podcast. Bernadettegallagher.blogspot.ie

Charlotte Gann is an editor from Sussex. Her poetry pamphlet *The Long Woma*n (Pighog) was shortlisted for the 2012 Michael Marks Award, and she has two collections published by HappenStance: *Noir* (2016) and *The Girl Who Cried* (2020). She is Convener of The Understory Conversation, an online hub for creatives.

Irene Garrow was born in Glasgow. She lives in London and has written a collection of poems and short stories. She works with prisoners to enhance their understanding of life and its challenges through shared reading of poems and stories.

Gillie Griffin moved to Canada from the UK in 1994, settling on the unceded traditional territories of the Algonquin people. After moving to Canada, her work in animal research ethics demanded much of her writing brain, but she continued to write poetry, publishing *Warm Bodies: Foreign Parts in the UK* with Loxwood-Stonleigh press. Home is now the village of Wakefield, Quebec, where she lives with one husband, one dog, and one cat; the other warm bodies having long since flown the nest.

Melanie Higgs is a freelance writer living on Vancouver Island, Canada, who only discovered the joys of writing poetry after retiring.

Mary-Jane Holmes lives, walks and writes in the wilds of the North Pennines. She has won the Live Canon Poetry Pamphlet Prize with her pamphlet *Dihedral*, the Bath Novella-in-Flash Prize (*Don't Tell the Bees*, published by Ad Hoc Fiction), the Bridport Poetry prize, Dromineer Flash Fiction Prize, Reflex Fiction Flash Fiction Prize and the Mslexia Flash prize. Her first collection of poetry, *Heliotrope with Matches and Magnifying Glass*, is published by Pindrop Press. She was a National Poetry Archive showcased poet during the lockdown.

Karin Andrews Jashapara has always written journals, poems and jottings for stories. For over thirty years, she wrote, designed and performed shadow theatre for adults and young people. Now she writes and draws; her current interests lie in heterotopic spaces and their imaginative and emotional potential. She also works as a Forest School leader and does spoken word storytelling.

Maria Jastrzębska is a poet, editor and translator. She was born in Warsaw, Poland and came to England as a child. Her most recent and fifth full-length collection is *Small Odysseys*, launched from Waterloo Press at the Coast is Queer Literature Festival in Brighton (2022). *The True Story of Cowboy Hat and Ingénue* (Cinnamon Press/Liquorice Fish, 2018) was her previous collection. She was the co-founder of Queer Writing South and South Pole and co-edited *Queer in Brighton*. She's also been the lead artist in an ACE awarded cross arts project Snow Q. mariajastrzebska.wordpress.com

Kavita A. Jindal is an award-winning novelist, poet and essayist. *Manual For A Decent Life* won the Eastern Eye Award for Literature (2020), was shortlisted for The Rabindranath Tagore Literary Prize (2021-2022), and as an unpublished manuscript, won the Brighthorse Prize in 2018. She has published three slim volumes of poetry: *Patina, Raincheck Renewed and Raincheck Accepted*. www.kavitajindal.com

Kathleen Jones is a poet and biographer living in the Lake District. *A Passionate Sisterhood*, her account of the sisters, wives and daughters of the Lake Poets won the Barclays Bank Prize for biography and was a Virago Classic. Her first collection of poetry, *Not Saying Goodbye at Gate 21*, won the Straid Award and was published by Templar. She is a committed environmentalist and organic gardener.

Sheena Joughin has published two novels and reviews fiction and memoirs for the *Times Literary Supplement*. She lives in West London with her cat, Ruby.

Avril Joy is an award-winning short story writer, novelist and poet. Before becoming a writer, she spent twenty-five years working in a women's prison. Her third novel, *A Little Madness in the Spring*, will be published in 2023 by Linen Press.

Crystal Z. Lee has called many places home, including Taipei, Shanghai, New York, and the San Francisco Bay Area. She explores her Taiwanese heritage, family history, and the places she's tethered herself to through her writing. An avid traveller, she is bilingual, speaking Mandarin and English. She is the author of two picture books and the novel *Love and Other Moods*.

S.J. Litherland's two poems come from her 8th collection in progress. Recipient of two Northern Writers Awards, she has twice won Commendations in the National Poetry Competition. Her latest book is *Composition in White* (2017) from Smokestack Books.

Marilyn Longstaff lives in Darlington and is a member of Vane Women. She has an MA in Creative Writing (University of Newcastle). Her poetry books are *Puritan Games*, *Sitting among the Hoppers*, *Raiment*, *Articles of War* (2017) and *The Museum of Spare Parts* (2018).

Victoria Maynard has been writing poems for the last ten years. Having grown up in Poland, the US and the UK, Vic's work centres on identity, the self and other, place and nature, and making sense of your ghosts. She currently lives in Brighton, pursuing a varied life involving writing, a MSc in psychology, and always the sea. She is working on her first poetry collection and can be found @vicamaynard

Deborah Morgan is from Liverpool, where she teaches Creative Writing. Her poetry has been published in *SPELT Magazine* and *London Grip*. Text was shortlisted for The Bridport Prize and published in *London Grip*. Deborah's first novel, *Disappearing Home*, was published by Tindal Street Press. The sequel, *Imagine Living*, will be available late in February 2023.

Ann Oakley is a writer and a sociologist. She is the author of many well-known academic publications on gender, women's health and social science. She has published essays, biographies, autobiographies, poetry and eight novels. Her latest book, *The Strange Lockdown Life of Alice Henry* (2022), was published by Linen Press. She enjoys playing with different forms of writing, and now, in her 80th year of writing, she plans to continue for as long as possible.

Jess Richards is the author of three literary fiction novels: Costa shortlisted *Snake Ropes*, *Cooking with Bones* and *City of Circles* (Sceptre). She also writes creative nonfiction, vispo, short fiction and poetry. Her most recent project is *Birds and Ghosts* (Linen Press), a book-length work of creative nonfiction.

Dr Khadija Rouf works for the NHS. She received commendations for short stories for the Manchester Fiction Prize (2016 & 2017). She is published in the NHS poetry anthology, These are *The Hands*, edited by Deborah Alma and Dr Katie Amiel. She has poems published in *Orbis*, *Sarasvati*, *Six Seasons Review* and *DreamCatcher*. Her poem, *Tacet*, was published in the Hippocrates Prize anthology (2021). She is also published in the The Whole Kahani's anthology, *Tongues and Bellies* (2022), published by Linen Press. Her poetry collection, *HouseWork* (2022) was published by Fair Acre Press.

Ali Rowland is a working-class poet, originally from Sheffield and now living in Northumberland. Ali writes from the perspective of mental health disability and has been published in *Up! Magazine*, *The Frogmore Papers* and *Obsessed with Pipework*.

Reshma Ruia is a writer based in Manchester. She is the author of two novels, *Something Black in the Lentil Soup* and *Still Lives*, as well as a short story collection, *Mrs Pinto Drives to Happiness*. Her poetry collection, *A Dinner Party in the Home Counties*, was awarded the Word Masala Award (2019). Her work has appeared in British and international journals and anthologies and has been commissioned by the BBC. She is the co-founder of The Whole Kahani writing collective. Find out more at www.reshmaruia.com

Holly Snaith writes for a living as a researcher and financial policy specialist (working for the House of Lords, Bank of England and HM Treasury, among others). At 31, she was diagnosed with bipolar disorder, which has inspired much of her subsequent prose and poetry (including an unpublished literary memoir, *The Disorder of Light and Dark*).

Gerry Stewart is a poet, creative writing tutor and editor based in Finland. Her poetry appeared as part of the iamb poetry project and on the *Eat the Storms* poetry podcast (2022). Her writing blog can be found at thistlewren.blogspot.fi and her Twitter @grimalkingerry

Eleanor Westwood lives in Devon and writes poems and short stories often inspired by local landscapes. Her poems have been published in *The Frogmore Papers*, *Earth Pathways Calendar* and *Diary*. *Being Beryl* was shortlisted for the Crediton Short Story Competition (2017). www.eleanorwestwood.co.uk

ACKNOWLEDGEMENTS

The Magic Coat, by Pen Avery, was first published online on her blog.

An earlier version of *Foundling* by Elizabeth Barrett was first published in *Yellow Nib*. No 11, (2016).

Beyond the Gate by Clare Best was published online in *The Friday Poem* (2021) and in *The Frogmore Papers* No.100, (2022).

My Mother with Sweet Peas by Clare Best was published in *The Frogmore Papers* No.93, (2019) and in her collection *Each Other* (Waterloo Press, 2019).

Unbound feet by Mona Dash was published in the anthology *Converse* (Pippa Rann Books, 2022).

Our Children's Childhoods by Charlotte Gann was first published online in *The Friday Poem*.

Clearing the Allotment by Gillie Griffin was first published online in the *Wandering Wakefield*, community blog.

Waiting Room by Mary-Jane Holmes was published in her collection *Dihedral* (Live Canon, 2021).

Petition by Mary-Jane Holmes was first published in *The Weardale Wordfest Anthology* (2022).

Awaiting Adoration by Kavita A. Jindal was first published in the anthology *Lips on Unfamiliar Skin* (The Writing Salon, 2021).

At Elephant Mountain by Kavita A. Jindal was first published in the anthology *Converse* (Pippa Rann Books, 2022).

Allotment by Kathleen Jones was published in her pamphlet *Hunger* (Maytree Press, 2022).

Dinosaurs by Marilyn Longstaff won The Holland Park Poetry and Politics Competition (2016) and is published online at *The Bakehouse*.

Text by Deborah Morgan was first published in *London Grip Magazine*.

An earlier version of *Daughter* by Khadija Rouf, was published in *Six Seasons Review* (2016)

Egg by Reshma Ruia was published in her collection, *A Dinner Party in the Home Counties* (Skylark Publications). The collection won the Word Masala Award (2019).

www.ingramcontent.com/pod-product-compliance
Lightning Source LLC
Chambersburg PA
CBHW041310110526
44590CB00028B/4310